Little People, BIG DREAMS™
NEIL ARMSTRONG

Written by
Maria Isabel Sánchez Vegara

Illustrated by
Christophe Jacques

Frances Lincoln
Children's Books

Little Neil was the eldest son of the Armstrongs, a family from Ohio, USA. He was just learning how to walk when his father took him to the Cleveland Air Races. Seeing the planes crossing the sky, he decided he wanted to become a pilot.

Neil was only six when he took his first plane ride. And on his 16th birthday he got the best present he could dream of: a license to fly. He earned it even before he could drive a car! It was later that month that he went on his first solo flight.

Wanting to learn everything about planes, Neil studied aeronautical engineering at university. But his studies were interrupted when he was sent to fight in the Korean War. After his aircraft was shot down, Neil was awarded three Air Medals for his bravery.

After the war, Neil completed his degree and became a hotshot test pilot. He flew the famous rocket-powered X-15 at almost 4,000 miles per hour, right to the edge of the atmosphere—just where the sky ends and space begins.

When he found out that NASA was looking for astronauts to command its first spacecraft mission, he sent an application. It arrived late, but a friend working there slipped it in the pile. He knew that Neil was perfect for the job... and he was right!

On his opening mission, Neil became the first person to connect a spacecraft to a rocket. Still, he almost lost his life when the tiny capsule span out of control. He had to make an emergency landing in the middle of the ocean.

His feat showed everyone at NASA that Neil had the experience, skills, and nerves of steel needed to lead the first spaceflight to the moon. Two other brave astronauts would join him: Buzz Aldrin and Michael Collins.

In July 1969, Neil and his teammates launched the Apollo 11 mission to the moon. As they lifted up, the spacecraft shook in every direction, just like the butterflies in their stomachs. But, once they reached space, everything went quiet.

It took them almost four days to reach the moon's orbit.
Michael stayed on the main spacecraft, while Neil and
Buzz jumped into the *Eagle*, their lunar module.

There were only thirty seconds of fuel left when they landed in the Sea of Tranquility, a dark plain that ancient astronomers mistook for an ocean.

The whole world was watching as Neil planted his left foot on the lunar surface and entered the pages of history as the first person on the moon.

It was one small step for a man
but a giant leap for humankind.

Back in the lunar module, they realized that the ignition button had broken. The most groundbreaking technology of the time had been used to take them there, but it was thanks to a pen jammed into the switch that they headed back home.

They returned to Earth as superstars! In New York, they were showered with ticker tape before they went on a victory lap around the world.

But to Neil, nothing felt better than going back to his
daily work dedicated to space exploration.

And today, Neil's footprints are still on the surface of
the moon, where there's no wind to disturb them—
the best tribute to a dreamer who knew that the
impossible can become reality with one small step.

NEIL ARMSTRONG

(Born 1930 – Died 2012)

1955

1958

Neil Armstrong was born in Wapakoneta, Ohio, on August 5th 1930, the eldest of three children. He fell in love with flying at a young age after visiting the Cleveland Air Races with his father. A keen Boy Scout, he earned his piloting license as a teen. Neil began studying aeronautical engineering at Purdue University, Indiana, but his studies were disrupted when he was drafted into the navy during the Korean War. After returning home to complete his degree, he began work as a civilian research pilot at NASA, the agency in charge of US space exploration, and in 1968, he joined its space program. During an early mission that almost ended in disaster, Neil became the first person to connect a spacecraft to a rocket. He was soon chosen to be the commander of Apollo 11, the first mission

1969

2009

to land humans on the moon. Alongside Buzz Aldrin and Michael Collins, he was launched into space, and the world held its breath as Neil became the first person to step foot on the moon on July 20th 1969. Neil and Buzz spent just under a day on its surface, collecting rock samples and taking photographs. When they returned to Earth, the astronauts were welcomed home as heroes. Neil received many awards, including the Presidential Medal of Freedom and the Congressional Space Medal of Honor. He largely stayed out of the public eye in later life. Instead, he began teaching and spent his days living on a dairy farm with his family. Neil will be forever remembered for humankind's first step into the unknown; a humble person who inspires us all to reach for the stars.

Want to find out more about **Neil Armstrong?**

Have a read of these great books:

I am Neil Armstrong by Brad Meltzer

Friends Change the World: We Are the Apollo 11 Crew by Zoë Tucker

Brimming with creative inspiration, how-to
projects, and useful information to enrich your
everyday life, quarto.com is a favourite destination
for those pursuing their interests and passions.

Text © 2022 Maria Isabel Sánchez Vegara. Illustrations © 2022 Christophe Jacques.
Little People Big Dreams and Pequeña&Grande are registered trademarks of Alba Editorial, SLU for books,
publications and e-books. Produced under licence from Alba Editorial, SLU.
First Published in the USA in 2022 by Frances Lincoln Children's Books, an imprint of The Quarto Group.
Quarto Boston North Shore, 100 Cummings Center, Suite 265D, Beverly, MA 01915, USA
Tel: +1 978-282-9590, Fax: +1 978-283-2742 **www.Quarto.com**

A catalogue record for this book is available from the British Library.
ISBN 978-0-7112-7103-6
Set in Futura BT.

Published by Peter Marley • Designed by Sasha Moxon
Edited by Lucy Menzies • Production by Nikki Ingram
Editorial Assistance from Rachel Robinson
Manufactured in Guangdong, China CC042022
1 3 5 7 9 8 6 4 2

Photographic acknowledgements (pages 28-29, from left to right): 1.Photograph of Neil Armstrong in the cockpit of the Ames Bell
X-14 airplane at NASA's Ames Research Center, Moffett Field, California, 1955. Image courtesy National Aeronautics and Space
Administration (NASA). © Smith Collection/Gado via Getty Images. 2. Portrait of Neil Armstrong in 1958, more than ten years
prior to the Apollo 11 mission in which he became the first human to set foot on the moon. The 30th anniversary of the Apollo 11
Moon landing mission is celebrated July 20, 1999. © NASA/Handout via Getty Images. 3. Neil Armstrong, Neil Armstrong In 1969,
Armstrong, An American Astronaut, Was The First Person To Set Foot On The Moon. © Encyclopaedia Britannica/UIG via Getty
Images. 4. UNITED STATES - JULY 21: Apollo 11 astronaut Neil Armstrong is introduced during the tribute event to the Apollo 11
astronauts celebrating the 40th anniversary of the first moon landing on Tuesday, July 21, 2009. © Bill Clark via Getty Images

Collect the Little People, BIG DREAMS™ series:

FRIDA KAHLO 	**COCO CHANEL** 	**MAYA ANGELOU** 	**AMELIA EARHART** 	**AGATHA CHRISTIE** 	**MARIE CURIE** 	**ROSA PARKS** 	**AUDREY HEPBURN**
EMMELINE PANKHURST 	**ELLA FITZGERALD** 	**ADA LOVELACE** 	**JANE AUSTEN** 	**GEORGIA O'KEEFFE** 	**HARRIET TUBMAN** 	**ANNE FRANK** 	**MOTHER TERESA** 
JOSEPHINE BAKER 	**L. M. MONTGOMERY** 	**JANE GOODALL** 	**SIMONE DE BEAUVOIR** 	**MUHAMMAD ALI** 	**STEPHEN HAWKING** 	**MARIA MONTESSORI** 	**VIVIENNE WESTWOOD** 
MAHATMA GANDHI 	**DAVID BOWIE** 	**WILMA RUDOLPH** 	**DOLLY PARTON** 	**BRUCE LEE** 	**RUDOLF NUREYEV** 	**ZAHA HADID** 	**MARY SHELLEY** 
MARTIN LUTHER KING JR. 	**DAVID ATTENBOROUGH** 	**ASTRID LINDGREN** 	**EVONNE GOOLAGONG** 	**BOB DYLAN** 	**ALAN TURING** 	**BILLIE JEAN KING** 	**GRETA THUNBERG** 
JESSE OWENS 	**JEAN-MICHEL BASQUIAT** 	**ARETHA FRANKLIN** 	**CORAZON AQUINO** 	**PELÉ** 	**ERNEST SHACKLETON** 	**STEVE JOBS** 	**AYRTON SENNA** 
LOUISE BOURGEOIS 	**ELTON JOHN** 	**JOHN LENNON** 	**PRINCE** 	**CHARLES DARWIN** 	**CAPTAIN TOM MOORE** 	**HANS CHRISTIAN ANDERSEN** 	**STEVIE WONDER** 

MEGAN RAPINOE

MARY ANNING

MALALA YOUSAFZAI

ANDY WARHOL

RUPAUL

MICHELLE OBAMA

MINDY KALING

IRIS APFEL

ROSALIND FRANKLIN

RUTH BADER GINSBURG

MARILYN MONROE

KAMALA HARRIS

ALBERT EINSTEIN

CHARLES DICKENS

YOKO ONO

MICHAEL JORDAN

NELSON MANDELA

PABLO PICASSO

AMANDA GORMAN

GLORIA STEINEM

FLORENCE NIGHTINGALE

HARRY HOUDINI

J.R.R. TOLKIEN

ELVIS PRESLEY

NEIL ARMSTRONG

ALEXANDER VON HUMBOLDT

ACTIVITY BOOKS

STICKER ACTIVITY BOOK

COLORING BOOK

LITTLE ME, BIG DREAMS JOURNAL

Discover more about the series at www.littlepeoplebigdreams.com